DO IT WITH DIGNITY

Do It with Dignity, A 30-day guide to help you let go of things and people that hold you back!

Julius Van Hook

November Media Publishing, Chicago IL.
Copyright © 2017 Julius Van Hook

All rights reserved. No part of this publication may be reproduced, distributed, or transmitted in any form or by any means, including photocopying, recording, or other electronic or mechanical methods, without the prior written permission of the publisher, except in the case of brief quotations embodied in critical reviews and certain other noncommercial uses permitted by copyright law. For permission requests, write to the publisher, addressed "Attention: Permissions Coordinator," at the email address below.
November Media
novmedia10@gmail.com

Ordering Information: Special discounts are available on quantity purchases by corporations, associations, and others. For details, contact the publisher at the email address above.
Printed in the United States of America
ISBN: 978-0-9981622-8-7

Cover Design: T Jones Media
Editing: Polgarus studio
Interior Design: Polgarus studio

I would like to dedicate the book to my grandparents, Mr. James and Mrs. Ora Gibson. Because of them, I am.

Contents

Be You 1
Treat Yourself Well 4
Find Peace Outside The Chaos 7
Keep Pushing The Limits 10
The Cycle Of Friendships 13
Live Above The Gossip 17
When People Show You Who They Are, Believe Them! 20
Don't Stay Trapped.. 23
Your Circle Will Get Smaller, Embrace It And Move On!.. 25
Validate Your Own Success 28
Give Thanks... 30
… And Lock The Door Behind You! 32
Know The Difference.. 34
It Is Worth The Price 36
Build Your Own Empire 39
Dream Killer 41
The Right People Will Come 44
Use Wisdom... 47

Business Is Just Business 49
You're Not The Only Peacemaker 51
The Truth 53
And We're Done 56
"Frenemy 101" 58
Keep Your Mouth Shut, And Save Your Dreams 61
Sometimes Proof Is Necessary 64
Dear Lord, Unplug Me From Unauthorized
Individuals Who Maliciously Drain Me! 67
If You Stand Still 70
Distance Yourself 72
Learn To Stand On Your Own 74
Self-Preservation 76

Day 1:
BE YOU

"Follow the Leader" was never a game I enjoyed growing up. I always felt as though it was some type of mind control game created to teach children at a young age that it's unacceptable to do anything outside of what you are told or taught. Now as an adult, I see the same thing happening in our society.

If our culture tells us that everyone is wearing purple on Fridays, I see a lot of individuals wearing purple faithfully every Friday. Culture tells us that it's in your best interest to color within the lines, I see a lot of folks falling to the ground and waddling in their failures because they tried to color outside the lines and enjoyed it until culture saw their masterpiece and condemned them for not following the rules. I know that just went over some of y'all heads… but I am going to keep it moving.

"Is being a follower beneficial to your existence?"

We were created to exist outside of the normalities of this world. If God wanted a nation where Hu-man was identical in all its characteristics and traits, don't you think He would have created us to carry all the same characteristics and traits?

"Stop letting culture dictate your role, position, and existence in the world!"

Being who you were created to be serves this country well. We need your creativity. We need your talents. We need your skills. We need your voice. And whoever tries to dim your light and tell you that you are shining too bright… it's not because they want you to necessarily follow them, it's because they are threatened by the amazing person God has created you to be.

"Be you fully, and unapologetically! The world will thank you later."

If you stay faithful and consistent to being who God has called you to be, in due time, it will pay off, and God will reward your courage!

Do It with Dignity!

Let go of all the expectations this world has put on you, and start learning and doing things that are beneficial for your existence.

Day 2:
TREAT YOURSELF WELL

I wish that I could stand at the top of the highest hill and scream this out loud so that everyone could hear me. However, since that's not going to happen, I need you to find a mirror, point to yourself and say it aloud for me: "It's not worth it!"

That bad relationship, that unstable friendship, that supervisor who finds every opportunity to call you out… is not worth the price of your piece of mind. In fact, I need you to put a stop payment on it right now!

"Stop investing in people, things, and situations that are not worth it!"

The truth is, toxic people exist and they will always exist. In fact, it seems as though if you get rid of one toxic person another toxic individual appears out of thin air. The next thing you know, you find yourself in the same situation, and believe me, this is not a coincidence!

You may have heard this a million times, but I feel compelled to remind you that you are the reason you are attracting these toxic individuals.

"Yes, you have encouraged the toxin!"

It is time to evaluate how much time and energy you are investing in toxic relationships, friendships, and situations. Because in all honesty, that same investment can go into you treating yourself like only God and you can do best.

"Loving yourself from the inside out!"

You have to start seeing the value and worth in your own life before you can expect someone else to see it and make the decision for themselves to say, "I am not going to bother _____ (insert your name) because I can see that _____ (insert your name) is not going to invest in my mess because _____ (insert your name) is too busy investing in_____(insert your name)'s mental, physical, and spiritual health."

Now I know what you're thinking. An individual who is full of mess will never admit to themselves that they are full of mess, like I just made them do above.

However, I can assure you that they will give a second thought to attaching themselves to you because believe it or not, people will begin to recognize that you are now investing in yourself and they will eventually move on to the next target. Yes, even the toxic people in your life currently. Why?

"Nothing can grow without being nourished!"

People will only treat you how you allow them to treat you. And the easiest way to hand over your energy, strength, time, emotions, and finances to someone not worth it… is by not investing those same things into something that is.

Do It with Dignity!

Start over! Today is a good day to start investing in you!

Day 3:
FIND PEACE OUTSIDE THE CHAOS

I've learned over the years that if you truly want to have meaningful relationships and friendships, you must stop investing in the wrong ones. I can almost bet that there are positive, inspiring, and loyal people in your life that you overlook on a consistent basis because all your time, energy, and devotion is being occupied by that friend or relationship that brings you the most chaos.

"You must stop investing in the chaos."

Bad relationships and bad friendships will suck the life out of you. They will drain you until you are unrecognizable and then after they have taken everything that they possibly can from you, they will demand even more time and energy, leaving you depleted and hopeless.

Meanwhile, there's that friend who answers the phone every time you call. Or there's that individual that you keep in the "friend zone," but you enjoy being around them because they understand you the most and they love you despite all your flaws. Yet those people in your life somehow always take the backseat, and you never recognize how valuable they are to you because you're so consumed with people, things, and situations that mean you no good.

"It's time to choose peace."

I feel like as humans we are were conditioned to be nurturers. Unfortunately, we want to care for and encourage the things and people that are the most harmful to us in hopes of changing them to fit into our lives. However, if we took that same principle and invested in people who loved us unconditionally, then we would be saying to ourselves, *I value peace and I will no longer accept anything less.*

If you want to stay focused and live a long, happy life, you must choose peace and pray for those who seek to deliberately use you and abuse you because only God can change them.

Do It with Dignity!

Do all that you can to preserve your peace of mind, and let go of the chaos.

Day 4:
KEEP PUSHING THE LIMITS

Why is it that people only seem to have something negative to say about you when you're striving to do better or you are becoming successful in a particular area of your life?

> **"Success and happiness seem to invite successful haters."**

Truthfully, the haters in your life would not have successful and thriving careers as haters if you did not give them the resources and tools they needed to succeed. Individuals who greatly dislike you or anything you are doing will always find the opportunity to point out everything you are doing wrong.

You started a business, but haters want to point out how whack your logo is. You wrote a book, but haters want to point out how whack your title is. You are in a successful, healthy relationship, but haters want to point out how your partner only has 50 followers on Instagram… Really?

"Hate on, haters!"

This only means that you are pushing the limits of your capabilities, and being true to yourself and who God has called you to be. And unfortunately, everyone is not going to celebrate this with you. Some people will either (A) be threatened by your success or (B) jealous of your success and happiness. Either way, you cannot let this discourage you, and you cannot afford to stop pushing for greatness.

"Never let anyone dim your shine!"

Yes, it may be true that some of the biggest doubters in your life are individuals who are close to you or whom you love the most. In fact, they are so good at hating on you that you start to wonder if you're doing too much or if you need to turn it down a notch so that it is not as offensive to them.

However, please don't be deceived. The moment you stop pursuing your dreams, or the moment you are back in the single person's club with them, they will still definitely have something else negative to say about that.

> **"People who hate on other people are never satisfied."**

You have to begin to recognize that people who are considered "haters" can never be pleased because of their own insecurities. So you have to make up in your mind that no matter who is riding with you, or who has your back… you're going to ride with yourself until the wheels fall off!

Do It with Dignity!

Keep pushing!

Day 5:
THE CYCLE OF FRIENDSHIPS

When I think of friendship, I reflect on that term totally differently than I used to when I was younger. Life has an interesting way of changing your perception of things. However, growing up I would consider anyone who was nice to me a friend, and if you were nice to me, always around and showed an interest in anything I was doing, then you were probably considered my best friend.

Now as an adult, the term friendship means something more endearing to me. In fact, because social media has made everybody and their momma friends, it's almost like you have to be intentional with defending the role of a friendship or else you will find yourself very disappointed when you realize that social media friendships are not something you should consider authentic or real.

The same could be said about a particular person in

your life whom you have considered a friend since grammar school.

Childhood friendships should definitely be re-evaluated in adulthood.

It's not to say that this person could not end up being a lifelong friend. However, you must ask yourself some key questions to help you determine if this is, in fact, a friendship you should continue to invest in as an adult. Especially since people can change over time, some for the better, others for the worse.

Question #1: Do we still share the same interests?

Sometimes this is not important if there is no expectation or requirements that suggest that you must share the same interests in order to remain friends. However, there should be some core interest that you have in common like religion, career, or lifestyle that keeps you both invested and connected. Without at least one core interest, you may not feel compelled to stay in touch. Let's be real, life happens, and you can barely keep up with your own family at times.

Question #2: Do you share the same values and principles?

It will be impossible to remain friends if you don't share the same values or even similar principles because someone is bound to get offended in this type of friendship. For example, if you don't think it's okay to live with the opposite sex before marriage and your friend has actually been living with his or her partner for the last six years, and they are not married, this may create tension. One friend may start feeling uncomfortable around and even avoiding the other, and how can you have a successful friendship like that? This brings me to my last question.

Question #3: Are you really friends?

Everyone has to outline what friendship looks like in their life. Some people value loyalty and respect, while others value time and commitment. Now don't get me wrong, neither are bad expectations. However, it's a good idea for you to understand that about yourself so that you can truly define who your genuine friends are and who your associates are.

If you value loyalty and respect, but you have a

friend who is always around or available to hang out, yet every time they come around they make you feel like crap because they judge you or point out all your flaws, it's probably best that you step away from investing in that friendship. If you can't be yourself with them, it is hurting you more to have them around.

Do It with Dignity!

Always remember that some people are in your life for a season. So be true to yourself and walk away from friendships that have passed their expiration dates.

Day 6:
LIVE ABOVE THE GOSSIP

There is life and death in our tongues. Our words have power. They can either edify others or destroy them. They can either blow out a fire or keep the fire burning. They can bring peace or start a war. So the thought-provoking question of the day is, how are you choosing to use your words?

I could go ahead and justify your pettiness and talk about how you need to ignore what other people are saying about you behind your back because they're just mad that they are not on your level. However, I want to encourage you to go a step further and live above the gossip.

I've seen relationships, friendships, marriages, and partnerships destroyed because individuals chose not to live above the gossip. Truthfully, we'd rather be upset, respond out of offense, and remove that person from our life.

"How can you live in peace and promote harmony if you lower yourself and retaliate to gossip?"

The best thing you can do to kill gossip, especially amongst family and friends, is to go to the individual who has started a rumor or talked about you behind your back and confront them face to face.

"It's hard to be the bigger person at times, but maturity always wins!"

Yes, being the bigger person takes courage and some level of maturity. And I would like to repeat this for those of you who'd rather not confront the other person. However, if you want to have peace in your life, it won't be good enough to simply ignore the other person and pretend that they do not exist. Especially if they are close to you.

Why? Because you will begin to harbor bitterness and hatred in your heart toward them. In fact, anytime someone mentions their name, you feel your heart starting to race. Now, what type of peace is this?

"Do your part, and then say goodbye if it's necessary."

It may be essential not to have this person in your life after you confront them. In fact, your objective doesn't even have to be restoration. But you owe it to yourself to address the issue, let the other individual know that you were offended by what they said, and then give them the opportunity to explain themselves or apologize.

If they cannot accept what you are saying, or still want to justify their behavior, then you should move on from that situation and let that person go.

Do It with Dignity!

Go in peace.

Day 7:
WHEN PEOPLE SHOW YOU WHO THEY ARE, BELIEVE THEM!

We've all heard the expression, fool me once shame on you, fool me twice shame on me. Well, recently I have had those words thrown back to my face because I wanted to believe the best in individuals very close to me. Yet, even after the truth was exposed, I still didn't want to believe what was unfolding before my eyes.

I found out that a few of my closest friends were actually liars and snakes. All this time I had been investing in what I thought was a genuine and authentic friendship, they were basically being disloyal to me.

Now I don't share this story with you to gain any type of empathy. I share this story with you because I want to help remove the blindfold from your eyes.

"Friends don't just wake up enemies. There was a malfunction from the beginning of the friendship!"

In your heart, you know who is real for you, but you just don't want to believe it. You feel like somehow what you heard, saw or felt was just a figment of your imagination, so you continued to ignore the signs of jealousy, lack of support, and dishonesty. Until one day the evidence becomes so overwhelming that you cannot ignore it any longer. However, my question is, why wait?

"Why do we wait until all the signs point to distrust and disloyalty?"

For most people it is an "I'll believe it once I see it" factor! But then when you see it, and the truth is actually revealed, you feel incredibly let down and disappointed because in a way you saw this coming.

However, do not be discouraged. For me, it was a tremendous opportunity for growth, and I have learned so much from this situation that will help me to make wiser decisions in the future. So though I may have lost a few friends along the way, what was meant for bad, God has allowed to be used for my good and His glory!

Do It with Dignity!

Don't look back! Always remember that some friends are just in your life to make you stronger.

Day 8:
DON'T STAY TRAPPED

When I have conversations with individuals who are bitter, frustrated, or even unpleasant to be around; eventually if I allow them to talk long enough, they always seem to slip up and reveal the source of their resentment through either verbal or nonverbal communication. Furthermore, through observation, I have learned that most unpleasant people have one major thing in common, and that is unforgiveness.

"Simply put, hurt people... hurt people."

When you hold on to what other people have done to you, you not only rob others of the opportunity to know you in a more loving, pleasant, and meaningful way, but you also extinguish knowing yourself in a more loving, pleasant, and meaningful way.

"Who are you?"

This issue at hand is, all you know is hurt, pain, and bitterness, so that is all you know how to give and attract. You walk around thinking that everyone is out to get you and that no one can be trusted, but please ask yourself, is this the way you want to live your life? Who did you once aspire to be, and why is that person not important enough to fight for?

"You must first love God, love yourself, and then forgive. In that order."

Yes, we don't know what you have been through or even how hard you were let down or disappointed by someone that you loved, respected, or trusted. However, losing your true identity is not worth the unforgiveness in your heart!

Do It with Dignity!

Stop punishing yourself and the world around you. Let go. Let God. Forgive.

Day 9:
YOUR CIRCLE WILL GET SMALLER, EMBRACE IT AND MOVE ON!

The hardest part about personal growth and development is realizing that your circle of friends will decrease dramatically, so please don't take it personally. The reality is that as we grow, God wants us to have people in our circle who will encourage this change and evolution, not hinder it.

"Your circle will be a reflection of either who you are currently or who you are striving to be."

So am I saying that you should personally go through a list of all your friends and mark off everyone who doesn't reflect where you are in life right now? Absolutely not! However, I will say that as you are going through life or different type of changes in your life, you will quickly realize who is really in your inner circle and who is not. Some of your friends will choose to leave your life voluntarily, or for others, it may just happen naturally because you will grow apart!

"Expect the unexpected."

Pay attention to the processes of elimination. More than likely, you will start losing friends at a very interesting time of your life. You will feel like things are either going really badly, or you may just be in a season where something has dramatically changed your life for the good or bad.

Nevertheless, the friends you thought would be there to ride or die with you will be nowhere to be found. However, don't take offense to this—I want you to realize that this is God's way of showing you who will be in your circle moving forward.

Truthfully, some people are only in your life when they feel like they can benefit from something you have going on. On the other hand, some people leave your life when they realize it is no longer all about them. Either Way, when you hit hard times or when their selfishness is revealed, they don't know how to handle it and eventually pull away from the friendship.

Do It with Dignity!

Don't cry over spilled milk! Recognize the good people you are surrounded by. Invest in those relationships and friendships. Move forward.

Day 10:
VALIDATE YOUR OWN SUCCESS

If you spend time looking for validation from other people, you will miss out on the opportunity to enjoy where you are in life and how much you have accomplished and grown.

> **"Everybody is not going to give you the congratulations that you are waiting for."**

Sometimes people will not recognize all your hard work until you're featured in a prominent magazine or interviewed by Oprah or Steve Harvey. However, in my opinion, that type of validation is good for the ego but not the soul.

If people cannot appreciate your grind and celebrate your little successes, then you probably don't need their support in the first place.

Also if you are only grinding hard to please other

people, then you will fail extremely fast when you realize that their support is only contingent on your performance.

"Self-validation is just as important as self-love."

I need you to go to a mirror and pat yourself on the back. YOU started that business. YOU closed the deals. YOU wrote your first book. YOU secured those speaking engagements. YOU went back to school. YOU stopped settling for less than what you are worth. So YOU give yourself a standing ovation. Skip what every once else thinks about you and validate yourself!

Do it with Dignity!

Stay true to yourself and know your own value!

Day 11:
GIVE THANKS

Sometimes when we move forward, and we are in a more *glorious season* of our lives, we tend to forget the things, people, and situations that helped push us to the very place we are today... and for some things in our past, we have every right to feel that way.

"I know that it's difficult to hold on to the past. Especially the seasons of hurt, pain, and shame."

In fact, I am spending a lot of time in this book encouraging you to forget the past and all the people who hurt you or let you down. And in all honesty, I am still encouraging you to do the same thing today.

Nonetheless, my objective today overall and with this entire book is to teach you how to do all things with dignity, integrity, and honor.

In fact, we must realize that everything... the good, the bad, and the ugly that has happened in our lives was for our good and has made us the people we are today.

> **"Without the rain, how could we appreciate the sunshine?"**

I'm not telling you to dwell on your past or soak in it. I am simply telling you to appreciate your past and be thankful that your past didn't take you out. Your past has made you stronger. Your past has made you wiser. God has allowed your past to build character in you that no man can take the credit for.

Do It with Dignity

In all things give thanks!

Day 12:
... AND LOCK THE DOOR BEHIND YOU!

We are constantly allowing negative things, people, and situations to walk in and out of our lives. Sometimes we are knowingly opening the door for this negativity and other times we are unaware of the negative things that we open ourselves up to. Either way, I am convinced that trouble doesn't last forever , and if you desire to be freed from these things, people, and situations that are holding you back or bringing you down... you can be set free!

"He will provide a way of escape."

However, the issue is not always the doors being closed... in my opinion, the issue that I see over and over again is the same doors that were just closed, being reopened!

- That bad relationships. Let it go!
- That broken friendship beyond repair. Let it go!
- That promotion you wanted but had to lie, steal, and cheat to get it, and it still didn't happen…. Let it go!

"You can't expect the wind to stop blowing, and the storm to stop raging in your home when you are keeping the door opened."

It's time to throw away the key, and it's time for you to move forward, walk forward, and get as far away from the negativity as you can. Stop praying for things to change and when they do you secretly desire the insanity again. There will always be an opportunity to experience peace in your life, family, marriage, business, or career. But you must allow some doors to be closed… and you must allow some doors to stay closed.

Do It with Dignity

Stop knocking on the same doors. If a door was closed that meant you no good, lock it and throw the keys away!

Day 13:
KNOW THE DIFFERENCE

They say, "All good things must come to an end," and for the most part that is a true statement. However, with friends and friendships, that doesn't always have to be the case, especially if you're mature enough to understand that not everyone will be your BFF.

"Some people in your life are only associates, so stop giving them promotions."

So what does this mean and how does this entire friendship theory play out for you? Well, for starters, don't be that open and vulnerable with everyone. If people want that type of friendship with you, let time, history, and loyalty establish itself first.

Next, don't do all the giving. If you're currently in a friendship and you find yourself giving the most time, energy, trust, and dedication, you will eventually be disappointed and begin to begrudge the friendship when you realize you're not getting the same thing in return.

> **"Pay close attention to the terms of your friendships with people. If you're the only one giving, step away from the situation."**

Lastly, if the induvial has a gazillion friends that they are very intimate with and share every emotional moment with, you need to start asking smart questions like, "How am I special?" It could be a case of social media stardom, and you're actually just another one of their fans!

Pay attention to the trend. How do you learn about most of the things going on in their life? Is it through an Instagram picture or Facebook post? Do they text you their deepest darkest secret, and then you read about it the next day on their blog? If so, it's pretty clear that they just consider you a fan, and chances are you might even just be their entourage. !

Do It with Dignity

Never confuse your associates with your ride or dies. Know the difference between those who are devoted to you and those who are just there for the ride.

Day 14:
IT IS WORTH THE PRICE

They say that anything worth having is definitely worth fighting for, and my friend… peace, joy, and happiness should unquestionably be added to that list.

One motivation for writing this devotional was to encourage you not to settle for any situations in life that would rob you of having the best life you could possibly have here on earth. But again, that is going to come with a price.

"Nothing is free!"

Yes, trials will come. Yes, heartache and pain will happen. Yes, there will be disappointments and letdowns. However, one thing should be consistent, and that is how you deal with the things in your life that come to take you out emotionally, physically, and mentally. Eventually, you will have to get to a place in your life where you are either a) unbothered or b) mature enough to rise above the negativity.

> **"Denying yourself of malicious ways and thoughts will be the price you will have to pay to achieve peace."**

Life will get tough, and things will fall apart sometimes; however, having peace in the midst of the storm will help you recover much faster.

One of the greatest quotes I have ever heard was spoken by the late Dr. Martin Luther King, Jr. and it truly changed my life forever. It stated:

> *"The ultimate measure of a man is not where he stands in moments of comfort and convenience, but where he stands at times of challenge and controversy."*

How we react to negative things in our life shows where we are mentally, spiritually, and emotionally. Now I am not saying that you will always react the right way, or that you will always do the right things or say the right things. Nonetheless, I think that it is important enough to consider.

Why live a life of frustration? Why allow people to bother you to the point of irritation? Why not have a life where every day when you wake up, your first words are of gratitude and not complaints?

We may not have the power to determine what happens in our life, but we have the power to decide how we are going to respond to the things that happen.

Do It with Dignity

Make up in your mind that the price of peace, joy, and happiness is worth it!

Day 15:
BUILD YOUR OWN EMPIRE

Over the last year or so, I have been very busy building my career and investing all I have into the man, brand, and professional that you see today. And one thing I have grown to realize and appreciate about this process is that it has taught me a lot about people and the road to success.

However, out of all the things I have learned, the one thing that stands out to me the most is the undeniable difference between people who "say" that they are building an empire compared to the people who are actually building an empire.

"It's impossible to watch and build at the same time. Keep your eyes on the things in your hands."

Stop with all the social media stalking and Facebook comparing, and focus on what's ahead for you. The more you consume yourself with other people's business, the less time you have to build yours.

"Outsmart your competitors with talent and skills, not unprofessionalism and pettiness."

Now I do believe in staying on top of the game with your competitors. It's perfectly normal to want to stay ahead of things in your career. However, there is a professional way that you can achieve this without becoming consumed or bothered by your competition.

I have come to realize that when I am consumed with others, I become less productive. I waste a large amount of my day being petty, complaining, or criticizing everything that others are doing… and believe it or not, that really does take up a lot of your day.

Do It with Dignity

Don't allow jealousy and competition to drive you. Stay focused, be consistent, and watch your own empire grow!

Day 16:
DREAM KILLER

Jealousy, envy, and malice… these are all dream killers. They will chew up your dreams and spit them back into your face. They will have you experiencing feelings of anxiety, fear, hopelessness, and even depression. So I caution you, in all that you do, guard your heart against these things.

I have seen it happen to far too many people, and in all honesty, these things have tried to creep up into my life as well. You're looking through social media and the next thing you know… someone has a new exciting career, a new companion, a new house or car and then you find yourself saying out loud, "Whatever, I can do better than that!"

"Don't become a hater!"

Yes, I am talking to you. Stop hating! Be happy for others in their season of joy and success because you will truly reap what you sow.

"Go ahead and shake off the saltiness."

In fact, you are going to get extremely mad at me for what I am about to say. However, jealousy is a condition of the heart. You don't just wake up with hatred and malice toward someone; that thing has been brewing for some time.

You need to forgive them for whatever you feel like they have done to you. Yes, the F word… Forgive. If they wronged you in the past, if they gossiped about you to other people, if they made an entire Facebook post about you without mentioning your name but you know that they were talking about you. FORGIVE! Why? Because you are only hurting yourself.

"Jealously, malice, and envy will keep you stuck and distracted."

While you are over there throwing a pettiness party, they are making moves! You have to understand that life is too short to waste it on being hateful toward someone else.

You never know what the other person had to endure to get the blessings they have. Don't gauge your happiness on other people's failures. Be happy for them, because what is for you, will be for you. However, you might just miss it because you're too distracted.

Do It with Dignity

Forgive. Move On. Be Happy.

Day 17:
THE RIGHT PEOPLE WILL COME

Sometimes it can feel a little bit overwhelming to maintain friendships in a technologically savvy generation. One minute you feel completely inspired by your friends and their accomplishments, and the next minute you're questioning if they are 100 percent for you after you feel the shade thrown your way through a social media update.

We're always questioning nowadays if our friendships are in fact authentic. Why? Because society has downgraded our friendship validation to a simple post, like, or page follow.

> **"We spend most of our time working hard for other to approve us via social media!"**

This foolishness really needs to stop, people. If someone makes you feel for any second that they are not for you, it is really time to cut the cord. However, do it with dignity, of course! Don't attack their character, or throw shade back at them. Just stop chasing that particular friendship.

I talk a lot about investing in friendships that are authentic, and now I want to encourage you to stop chasing friendships that you always have to question.

"If someone is a true friend, history and time will reveal it!"

I try not to create relationships in my head simply because someone follows my Facebook page, likes all my posts, and shares my content every once in a while. I also don't consider everyone that I partner with or do business with my friend.

"It is what it is!"

Everyone plays a role in your life. So don't confuse them! Keep working hard, mind your own business, and if you pay close attention to the individuals in your life, you will discover who your real friends are.

Do It with Dignity

Don't be discouraged—the right people for you will come and stay!

Day 18:
USE WISDOM

"In life, you will have moments and seasons of weakness; that is just a fact of life."

Truthfully, we all have things we battle in our minds and hearts that can knock us to our knees in a humbling way. Nevertheless, what makes these seasons even more depressing or difficult is when you feel as though you have to go through them alone.

"But who can you really trust?" you ask!

I agree. It's hard to make yourself vulnerable to others, especially if you are not sure if they will later use your weaknesses for their gain and glory. Yet, I am not a huge advocate for enduring tough moments and situations by yourself.

"Don't go through a trial alone—use wisdom and open up to the people who are really in your corner."

One of the biggest ways to heal during difficult times is with the edification and encouragement of those who really care about you in spite of your status, financial situation amount of money, or what you can do for them.

Those individuals will be the ones who call to check on you even when you don't have anything exciting going on. Those individuals will be the ones who come over to hang out and don't expect you to pick up the tab all the time. Those people will be the individuals who pray with you or for you on a consistent basis.

Do It with Dignity

"Lead with your heart, not your convenience."

Don't just open up to the first person who calls you on a daily basis. Pray about it, pay attention to the positive habits of people around you, narrow down your friend list outside of difficult seasons, and follow your heart.

Day 19:
BUSINESS IS JUST BUSINESS

The quickest way to be disappointed in an individual is to assume that what you have together is more than what you really have. Whether it is a friendship or a romantic relationship with someone, you naturally only get hurt by people you have specific expectations for.

Truthfully, I see this the most in professional, business or work relationships! An illusion of friendship takes place while working on projects or spending time together in the same office space, so you end up sharing personal stories, common goals, dreams and aspirations with people that you would normally never be vulnerable with.

The next thing you know, while you are planning to take over the world with them, you feel completely blindsided when they throw you under the bus, move on, or take full credit for a project that you have been working on together since day one.

> **"You must be careful… there are a lot of wolves wearing sheep's clothing."**

In fact, the simple rule to remember is that everyone who smiles to your face is not always for you. There is no loyalty required of a professional, business, or work relationship. Yes, true friendships can develop. However, you should always keep things in perspective.

> **"The only thing you both have in common at the moment is seeing a product or vision come to life… nothing more, nothing less."**

Do It with Dignity

Always keep things in perspective. Develop friendships when it's time to develop friendships. Do business when it's time to do business.

Day 20:
YOU'RE NOT THE ONLY PEACEMAKER

I am a huge fan of forgiving, letting go, and moving on. On the other hand, I am not at all a fan of playing anybody's fool.

I don't have time to keep letting history repeat itself because I have too many things to be doing and accomplishing than to continue to deal with your lies, dishonesty, cheating, or whatever it is I have forgiven you of in the past.

"Doing the same thing over and over is foolish!"

I hear a lot of people say that the good thing to do is to keep loving, keep praying, and keep forgiving. And though I do agree with those ideologies, I also believe that at some point you need to stop being everyone else's peacemaker, and focus on finding your own peace!

"While you are trying to keep the peace for everyone else... who is keeping the peace for you?"

Who is staying up late at night to dry your tears? Who is coming over to cater to your home while you try to keep the peace in others? Who is sacrificing for you when you have given your last?

Now I know this sounds punitive, but in theory, it's not. I am just encouraging you to look at the situation fully. If you are the one that everyone is walking over, if you are the one that everyone is mistreating, if you are the one that everyone is misusing, then you are not at peace.

Do It with Dignity

Yes, do forgive! Yes, do move on! No, don't play anybody's fool!

Day 21:
THE TRUTH

Have you ever questioned a chair that you were about to sit in? Did you look at the chair and say, "Please don't let me down!" Nope! You just sat your happy self down in the chair and trusted that it was going to hold you up and not crumble underneath you.

That is what trusting something wholeheartedly feels like. You don't have an ounce of doubt in your heart. You believe without questioning, and you hope without someone having to tell you.

In fact, if I stay with the same analogy of the chair, even if you saw a chair that was broken down and thrown to the side, if someone came and fixed it you would sit in the chair again with the same trust and assurance that you would give any other chair. Why? Because you know that a chair was created to hold you. No questions asked, and this should be exactly how real love and trust feels in your life.

"You should never need to question the individuals in your life who say that they love you... even when the relationship has been broken and put back together."

Nevertheless, how do you get to this place of recognizing that type of love in your life? How do you trust their love for you, especially after the trust was broken?

This is a great question; however, I think it's the wrong question to ask initially. The better question to ask is, "What is this person's purpose in my life?"

It's easy to trust a chair because we know the purpose of the chair. So even if it breaks down and is fixed again, because we know its purpose—as long as it is operating like a chair, we know that we can trust it.

Now you might think I am going too far with this chair theory, but consider this last thing about the chair and I will let it go, *I promise*! But think about this: if the chair starts portraying itself as a bookshelf, now we have a real issue. Why? Because we have different expectations for a bookshelf.

In fact, I think I have a right to question the chair, who is portraying itself as a bookshelf. And I also have a right not to trust that chair any longer. Truthfully, I don't think I will ever sit in that chair again.

The same principle applies to people in your life. Ask yourself important questions. What is the role of this person in my life, and are my expectations for them exceeding their requirements? If you do not ask this question first, you will always be questioning their intentions and motives.

> **"No one can love perfectly, but real love never fails."**

Do It with Dignity

Stop questioning *truth* and *love*, and let them speak for themselves.

Day 22:
AND WE'RE DONE

Dealing with bitter, emotionally immature people is poisonous. Every time you see this person, there is always an issue with YOUR behavior and YOUR actions—and according to them, you can't seem to do anything right.

They always find a reason to get in your face and confront you about something that you are doing or not doing, and the interaction is always awkward and messy!

This individual cannot seem to let go of the past or any mistakes that you have made. They have a million and one questions, and try to belittle you in front of everyone all the time. Then they want to throw in the highly-misrepresented statement… "I'm just playing" when everyone knows that after their accusations, there is nothing funny about their remarks.

Now you're 100 percent annoyed and frustrated with the individual, and you are ready to explode. However, in this situation, don't even waste your emotions. I need you to just step back and say….

"…And we're done!"

Yes, just like that. Stop letting people interrupt your life with their immature, petty behavior!

Go ahead and try it….

> *Them: Why didn't you like my Facebook post but you liked x,y,z's post?*
> *Me: Petty… so we're done!*
> *Them: Why didn't you come to my sixth business launch party the other day?*
> *Me: I'm sorry I had to miss this one, even though I've been to the last five.*
> *Them: You're just jealous!*
> *Me: Petty… so we're done!*

It is that simple, and trust me when I say the sooner the better!

Do It with Dignity

Stop trying to figure out emotionally immature people. They will drag you under. Stop explaining yourself and just be done.

Day 23:
"FRENEMY 101"

To trust or not to trust is always the question with friends who are secretly praying for your empire to fall! These people are only standing around waiting for the moment you crumble and are doing either as bad or worse than they are.

They are patting you on the back one day, and stalking you on social media the next day to see what moves you are making.

"I say to these people all the time, stop getting in my business and mind yours!"

Nevertheless, these individuals exist, and we call them frenemies. Frenemies will call you every day, come to your house weekly, and show up at all your events… just to see what you are up to and how they can either gain from your success or outdo you later. But don't be foolish! Pay attention to your entourage!

"Everyone is not for you, and if you look closely, you can spot them right away."

Sign #1: They are always around complaining about how bad they have it.

We all know that everyone has bad days. However, the "woe is me" movement is a force like none other! These people get easily jealous of others and look for opportunities to blame everyone else for their failures.

Sign #2: They are always giving you compliments… ALWAYS!

Now don't get me wrong, encouragement and edification is a plus in friendships. I personally enjoy when my friends take notice of my accomplishments and celebrate with me. However, that friend who is always saying how you have your life together, and how their life sucks, is probably not giving you a real compliment; I mean how could it be if they make you feel bad for them right after they compliment you? Just think about it!

Sign #3: They are always trying to get you to collaborate with them.

I hate opportunists! Now again, a good partnership can be an advancement for the both of you. However, let's say you collaborate and the venture fails… then all of a sudden, they have an attitude with you and are making weird statements like, "You didn't give this your all!" Why? Because you were supposed to be their ticket to success.

Sign #4: They are MIA as soon as they start winning!

What? Where are you? Crickets….

Do It with Dignity

Be careful who you are connecting with and letting in your inner circle!

Day 24:
KEEP YOUR MOUTH SHUT, AND SAVE YOUR DREAMS

"Don't let your left hand know what your right hand is doing!"

I know that most of you reading this book have heard this very prudent scripture recited back to you at some point during your existence… yet a lot of us still can't get this practical principle right.

"Stop running your mouth!"

Simply put, if you are tired of feeling like people are out to get you or sabotage the gifts and dreams that you have, don't keep running your mouth to everyone about the things you have going on or the things you are planning to do in the future.

"Sometimes it's okay to dream alone!"

I don't care if it's your momma, daddy, sister, brother, next-door neighbor, coworker, etc., please be vigilant with who you are telling your business to.

"Some people are just investigating so that they can cause an interruption in your plans."

I have made it a legit habit not to say anything about what I am doing until it's done or I am confident that nothing will stop me. This way, it's way too late for the doubters to talk me out of it, it's way too late for the haters to hate, and it's way too late for the naysayers to say, "Yeah right, that will never happen!"

"The only thing I want to leave people with is an opportunity to say well done!"

Opening your mouth too soon and disclosing great ideas, dreams, and visions can be very destructive to your future. There are real people in your life who are only put there to disrupt your dreams and visions.

Do It with Dignity

Keep some things to yourself!

Day 25:
SOMETIMES PROOF IS NECESSARY

I am a firm believer that individuals who want to be a part of your life will go out of their way to prove it! Conscientiously speaking, no one is perfect, and we all fall short at times. Yet, there should be some type of indication that your friends or companions support you, are there for you during both tragedy and triumph, and have your back, side, front, and middle 100 percent!

"Don't be misled; it's absolutely about who walked into your life and said, 'I'm here for you' and proved it."

The number one question people ask all the time, whether indirectly or not, is, "How do you know if someone in your life is meant to be there?" Nevertheless, if I had to answer the question for them,

I would respond by asking them another question in return: "Have you seen any proof that they are emotionally invested and want to be there?"

"People will eventually show their true colors. So, when they show you, believe them!"

Now, of course, no one is faultless. There will be moments in every relationship or friendship where disappointment, arguments, and frustrations will occur. However, do not confuse those moments with growing pains.

If you are always fighting, not seeing eye to eye, or can't stand the sight of one another, it's not petty for you to think that something is not right, but it's called insight. The truth is, after all is said and done, does reconciliation truly take place?

As I mentioned a hundred times throughout this 30-day guide, if you ever question someone's position in your life, then there may not be enough proof that they are actually for you.

Do It with Dignity

Check the proof sheet, believe the facts, and make a clear assessment. If you have any doubts, you may not have enough evidence of a real friendship or relationship.

Day 26:
DEAR LORD, UNPLUG ME FROM UNAUTHORIZED INDIVIDUALS WHO MALICIOUSLY DRAIN ME!

Protect your sanity, protect your joy, protect your peace of mind. Guard them with your life and then pray that God shields all the unseen expanses, because there are malevolent people in this world whose only objective is to bring you down to their deplorable level.

"Unhappiness thoroughly enjoys company."

Let me just say that a miserable person will do everything in their power to bring you down, steal your joy, and destroy your momentum… and they will do it intentionally if you allow them! However, it is your responsibility to protect your space and your positive energy, and here are three simple directives to help you do that more effectively.

Do It with Dignity

First, listen to them vent about their problems with an open ear and not an open heart.

Don't take on anyone's insecurities, worries, doubts, or ungratefulness. This is how you will find yourself entangled in your mind and heart. Their problems are not your problems. Their concerns are not your concerns. Pray for them, but guard your heart so that you don't start developing the same insecurities, worries, or doubts.

Second, give to others out of your abundance, not lack of....

This concept is simple. If you don't have anything to give, do not allow anyone to make you feel bad, especially after you have given all that you have.

Third, stop feeling guilty for saying NO, and practice saying NO more often.

People will abuse your generosity and take advantage of your incapability to say NO. However, it is your right to say NO. Also, it is your right not to feel obligated to explain why you said NO.

"Only allow God to use you!"

Day 27:
IF YOU STAND STILL

*"Let God fight your battles. To win,
all you have to do is be still!"*

I think that every mother or even grandmother in an African-American family has quoted this scripture to her child or grandchild at one point in their life, and this is absolutely a principle that I try to stand on daily.

I don't have time to worry about any of my enemies, and I don't have time to plot and plan the destruction of another man because I am too busy enjoying my life and preparing for my future.

"The greatest way to give someone victory in your life who is praying for your destruction is to surrender your time, energy, and resources to them."

When you ignore your haters, and keep living life as normal or even better than normal—you have defeated their feeble attempt to bring you down.

"Your happiness, peace of mind, and genuine joy are all weapons that can cause even your enemies to surrender."

To stand still and be unbothered by what others are doing or saying to you takes more strength, power, and courage than retaliation.

Do It with Dignity

So, don't be afraid of foolish men or women. Stand still and be patient. God will most definitely show up right on time!

Day 28:
DISTANCE YOURSELF

I have always wondered if you could trust a person who gossips and talks about everyone around them. Honestly, I can understand that in most situations it can seem innocent and playful. However, one should really sit back and think about whether this type of person can really be of value to you in a friendship.

It's almost the same scenario as a relationship brought together through infidelity. We often ask men or women who are in a relationship now with an individual who left someone else to be with them, "Do you really think that this person can be loyal to you when clearly they have an issue with commitment, honesty, and faithfulness?"

The same questions can be asked of someone who has a friend or friends who gossip about everyone.

"Do you really think that this person is not talking about you to others, when clearly they

have an issue with slander, defamation of character, and loyalty?"

In fact, either one of two things can be concluded from this type of friendship. (A) you're just as bad of a gossiper as they are and in that case, you should not be surprised when you hear about them throwing you under a bus to someone else. Or, (B) you clearly need to change your association… because gossip is like a poison and it will eventually start to destroy everything living and thriving around it.

Do It with Dignity

Change your association and delete poisonous and toxic people from your circle!

Day 29:
LEARN TO STAND ON YOUR OWN

Some of the best times in my life were when I was at peace with who I was. The air around me blew a little cooler. The sky above me seemed a little brighter, and the grass underneath me appeared a little greener. Happiness, peace, and joy were in my left hand—and success, longevity, and endurance in my right.

The point I am trying to make is that being at peace with who you are makes a tremendous difference in the way that you perceive the world around you. Yes, heartache, disappointment, and suffering may occur in life. Yes, people will come and go who mean you no good; however, when you learn to stand on your own despite what is going on around you, things begin to shift in your favor.

You find yourself putting aside the expectations of others, you begin to develop a heart of gratefulness because you're not comparing your life to someone else's, you are content with where you are because you know that this is not your end. You begin to live each day like it is your last, and you find appreciation in everything and everyone around you.

"Learning to stand on your own doesn't mean you live a life of isolation; however, it means that you live a life of purpose, fulfillment, and peace outside of the extent of this society."

You will begin to understand that other people's opinion of you no longer matter. In fact, you will find yourself wishing happiness, love, peace, and joy to all men, even your enemies. Why? Not because you are weak or oblivious, but because you are strong and confident and you know your place in this world without validation.

Do It with Dignity

Know yourself, be yourself, and free yourself. Get comfortable with standing alone, or be content with blending in.

Day 30:
SELF-PRESERVATION

If there is one message I would like you to receive loud and clear from this 30-day guide… it is the message of self-preservation. If you do not protect yourself from things that can harm or damage you mentally, spiritually, emotionally, or physically, then destruction will occur.

Essentially, outside of God, you and only you have the power to overcome things and situations that try to tear you down, and I hope that you realize this after reading my book.

"Change starts with you!"

In order to make some tangible changes in your life, you will need a strategy to assist you with getting rid of all the negativity and garbage deposits that people have dumped on you for years and years.

Whether that is cutting some people loose, investing in yourself, or shutting some doors you keep opening in your life that are not beneficial….

"YOU WILL NEED TO TAKE ACTION and stop waiting for someone else to solve your problems."

In fact, I want to leave you with no more excuses and no more opportunities to point the finger at circumstances, situations, or people. There is absolutely nothing or no one on this earth that can hold you down, but yourself!

Do It with Dignity

Don't wait until the first day of the year to get it right. Today is your New Year! Hit the restart button, make some resolutions and go forward!

www.ingramcontent.com/pod-product-compliance
Lightning Source LLC
Chambersburg PA
CBHW050544300426
44113CB00012B/2252